on every page

Chloe & Ben

Bake your way to Christmas

with Kiddi Caru
and Dicky Birds

Written by
Caroline Meek

Illustrated by
Sarah-Leigh Wills

Welcome to
Kiddi Caru and Dicky Birds Day Nurseries'
Christmas Recipe Book

Chloe and Ben love to bake. Every Christmas when their family and friends gather to celebrate, everyone brings their favourite homemade treats. Chloe and Ben would like to share some of their family's favourite recipes with you. Enjoy making these delicious treats with your loved ones.

Contents

Don't forget to...

SPOT ROO AND CHARLIE on every page

Guide for grown-ups

We hope you enjoy making these recipes with your child. As you prepare and bake your Christmas treats, give your child lots of opportunities to help. Ask them to find ingredients and utensils, and encourage them to mix ingredients and stir.

When it is safe to do so, allow them to feel the texture of the mixture. Make sure they don't have access to anything sharp, heavy or hot. Children should be supervised at all times.

Before you start, make sure you and your child do these simple tasks:

• Wash your hands.

• Tie back loose hair.

• Read the recipe together from start to finish.

• Find all the ingredients you will need, and measure them out.

• Protect your clothes with an apron.

Auntie Aashi's Fruitcake

Preparation time: 15 minutes

Cooking time: 30 minutes

Serves: 8-10

Ingredients:

- 150g (5oz) self-raising flour
- 150g (5oz) caster sugar
- 150g (5oz) butter
- 3 large eggs
- 85g (3oz) mixed fruit or raisins

You will need:

Baking paper

Bowl

Wooden spoon

Round cake tin
(5–6 inch in diameter)

Let's get ready

1. (GU) Preheat the oven to fan 160°C/180°C/350°F/gas mark 4.
2. Line the cake tin with baking paper.

Let's get baking

1. Put the sugar and butter in a bowl. Mix them together using a wooden spoon.
2. We recommend that you crack the eggs into a separate bowl (to check that no shell gets in the bowl) before adding them to the mixture.
3. Add the eggs to the mixture. Mix again for approximately 1 minute.
4. Add the flour, and mix until you have a smooth batter.
5. Stir in the fruit until it is evenly distributed.
6. Place the mixture in a cake tin.
7. (GU) Bake for 25–30 minutes until golden brown.
8. (GU) Allow to cool in the cake tin, then carefully remove the baking paper and place the cake on a wire rack or plate.

● ● ● ● ● ● ● ● ●

Let's get tasting

(GU) To serve, add a drizzle of warm vanilla custard to a slice. Enjoy!

Granny Susan's Flapjacks

Preparation time: 15 minutes

Cooking time: 25 minutes

Makes: 15

Ingredients:

- 90g (3oz) butter
- 90g (3oz) brown sugar
- 50ml (3 tbsp) golden syrup
- 195g (6¾oz) oats

You will need:

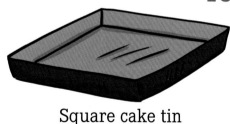

Square cake tin
(5-6 inch in diameter)

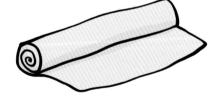

Baking paper

Wooden spoon

Saucepan

Let's get ready

1. **(GU)** Preheat the oven to fan 160°C/180°C/350°F/gas mark 4.
2. Line the cake tin with baking paper.

Let's get baking

1. **(GU)** Melt the butter, sugar and golden syrup in a saucepan.
2. **(GU)** Stir until the sugar is dissolved.
3. **(GU)** Add the oats and mix well. Once they have been mixed in, remove from the heat.
4. **(GU)** Spoon the mixture into the cake tin. Bake for around 20–25 minutes or until golden brown.
5. **(GU)** Allow to cool in the cake tin, then turn out the flapjacks onto a flat surface and remove the baking paper.
6. **(GU)** Cut the flapjacks into 1-inch squares.

● ● ● ● ● ● ● ● ●

Let's get tasting

(GU) Feeling adventurous? Drizzle melted chocolate over the flapjacks before allowing them to cool. Enjoy!

Chloe and Ben are having fun with their friends Anya and Max, baking in the nursery kitchen with Carlos.

But they're missing some of the things they will need to bake a cake!

8

Cousin Laila's Fruit and Oat Cookies

Preparation time: 15 minutes
Cooking time: 12 minutes
(plus 1 hour in the fridge)
Makes: 18

Ingredients:

- 75g (2½oz) butter
- 65g (2¼oz) caster sugar
- 125g (4½oz) self-raising flour
- 1 large egg
- 45g (1½oz) dried fruit of your choice (e.g. raisins, apricots, cranberries)
- 60g (2oz) oats

You will need:

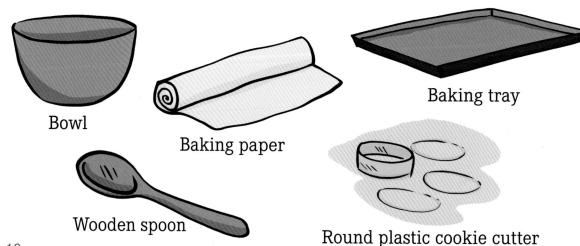

Bowl

Baking paper

Baking tray

Wooden spoon

Round plastic cookie cutter

Let's get ready

1. (GU) Preheat the oven to fan 155°C/175°C/345°F/gas mark 3.
2. Line the baking tray with baking paper.

Let's get baking

1. Mix together the caster sugar and butter in a bowl.
2. We recommend that you crack the eggs into a separate bowl (to check that no shell gets in the bowl) before adding them to the mixture.
3. Add the egg, flour, oats and fruit, then mix to form a dough.
4. Place the dough in the fridge for an hour to firm.
5. Lightly dust the worktop or table with flour, then roll out the dough to just over the thickness of a £1 coin and cut it into circles using a cutter.
6. Add the mixture to the tray.
7. (GU) Bake on the middle shelf of the oven for 10–12 minutes.
8. (GU) Allow to cool.

• • • • • • • •

Let's get tasting

(GU) Why not pour a glass of cold milk to drink with your cookie? Enjoy!

11

Grandpa Sid's Cocoa Rice Pudding

Preparation time: 5 minutes

Cooking time: 40 minutes

Serves: 5

Ingredients:

- 38g (1¼oz) pudding rice
- 300ml full-fat milk
- 15g (½oz) caster sugar
- 1 tsp cocoa powder
- Berries (e.g. blueberries, raspberries)

You will need:

Sieve

Dessert bowls

Wooden spoon

Saucepan

Let's get ready

1. Wash the rice thoroughly under cold water in the sieve, until the water runs clear.

Let's get baking

1. (GU) Add all the ingredients to the saucepan, apart from the berries, then slowly bring the mixture to a boil, stirring often.
2. (GU) When it starts to boil, reduce the heat and allow to simmer for 30–40 minutes, or until the rice is cooked.
3. (GU) Add more milk to thin down the rice pudding if it gets too thick.
4. (GU) When it's cooked, spoon the mixture into dessert bowls and top with berries.

● ● ● ● ● ● ● ●

Let's get tasting

(GU) If you fancy a festive flavour of rice pudding for Christmas, why not use cinnamon instead of cocoa? Enjoy!

Chloe and Ben and their friends Anya and Max have made a mess in the nursery kitchen. It's time for them to clean up.

Help them find the tools they'll need to make the kitchen sparkling clean.

Nana Mona's Jam Tarts

Preparation time: 20 minutes
Cooking time: 15 minutes
Makes: 20

Ingredients:

- 500g (1lb 2oz) sweet shortcrust pastry
- Butter for greasing the tin
- Flour for sprinkling
- Jam (apricot, blackcurrant or strawberry)

You will need:

Round plastic pastry cutter

(plus a cutter in a different shape, for decorating. We like star and heart-shaped cutters)

Rolling pin

Fork and spoon

Mini-muffin tins

16

Let's get ready

1. **(GU)** Preheat the oven to fan 180°C/200°C/400°F/gas mark 6.
2. Grease the mini-muffin tins with butter.

Let's get baking

1. Roll out the shortcrust pastry onto a lightly floured surface until it's just under the thickness of a £1 coin.
2. Stamp out twenty 5cm circles using a pastry cutter.
3. Place the pastry circles in the muffin tin.
4. **(GU)** Prick each circle with a fork several times.
5. Spoon 1 tsp of jam into each.
6. Roll out the leftover pastry. Stamp out shapes to decorate the tarts using your other cutter(s).
7. **(GU)** Bake the tarts in the oven for 12–15 minutes, until the pastry is golden.
8. **(GU)** Allow to cool. Check that the jam is cold before eating.

• • • • • • • • •

Let's get tasting

Why not try filling your tarts with different jams to give your guests a choice of flavours and a beautifully colourful serving? Enjoy!

Uncle Tarik's Chocolate and Cherry Cake

Preparation time: 15 minutes

Cooking time: 30 minutes

Serves: 8

Ingredients:

- 200g (7oz) self-raising flour
- 100g (3½oz) caster sugar
- 100g (3½oz) sunflower oil
- 3 large eggs
- 100g (3½oz) cherries
- 20g (½oz) cocoa powder
- milk (as needed)

You will need:

Wooden spoon

Baking paper

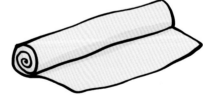

A cake tin or a baking tray and cupcake cases

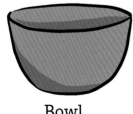

Bowl

Let's get ready

1. (GU) Preheat the oven to fan 160°C/180°C/350°F/gas mark 4.
2. If you're using a cake tin, line it with baking paper.

Let's get baking

1. Place all the ingredients, except the cherries, in a bowl and mix together. If the mixture is too thick, add some milk.
2. Fold in the cherries, then spoon the mixture into the cake tin or cupcake cases.
3. (GU) Bake in the oven for 15–20 minutes for cupcakes, or 25–30 minutes in a cake tin.
4. (GU) The sponge is ready when it springs back when you press it in the middle.
5. (GU) Allow to cool in the cake tin or cupcake cases, then turn out onto a wire rack or plate.

• • • • • • • • •

Let's get tasting

Try topping your cake with some fresh berries and a sprig of mint. Enjoy!